LAKE DISTRICT

A POCKET ALBUM

Adapted from an original book by
ROLY SMITH

First published in the United Kingdom in 2004 by
The Francis Frith Collection

This large print edition published in 2017 by Black Horse Books,
an imprint of The Francis Frith Collection
ISBN 978-1-84546-819-4

British Library Cataloguing in Publication Data

Lake District—A Pocket Album
Adapted from an original book by Roly Smith

The Francis Frith Collection
19 Kingsmead Business Park, Gillingham
Dorset SP8 5FB UK
Tel: +44 (0) 1722 716 376
Email: info@francisfrith.co.uk
www.francisfrith.com

Printed and bound in Great Britain

Front Cover: Coniston, **WATERHEAD 1912** 64281t
The colour-tinting is for illustrative purposes only, and is not intended to be historically accurate.

AS WITH ANY HISTORICAL DATABASE THE FRITH ARCHIVE IS CONSTANTLY
BEING CORRECTED AND IMPROVED AND THE PUBLISHERS WOULD WEL-
COME INFORMATION ON OMISSIONS OR INACCURACIES

CONTENTS

FRANCIS FRITH
VICTORIAN PIONEER

Francis Frith, founder of the world-famous photographic archive, was a complex and multi-talented man. A devout Quaker and a highly successful Victorian businessman, he was philosophic by nature and pioneering in outlook. By 1855 he had already established a wholesale grocery business in Liverpool, and sold it for the astonishing sum of £200,000, which is the equivalent today of over £15,000,000. Now in his thirties, and captivated by the new science of photography, Frith set out on a series of pioneering journeys up the Nile and to the Near East.

INTRIGUE AND EXPLORATION

He was the first photographer to venture beyond the sixth cataract of the Nile. Africa was still the mysterious 'Dark Continent', and Stanley and Livingstone's historic meeting was a decade into the future. The conditions for picture taking confound belief. He laboured for hours in his wicker dark-room in the sweltering heat of the desert, while the volatile chemicals fizzed dangerously in their trays. Back in London he exhibited his photographs and was 'rapturously cheered' by members of the Royal Society. His reputation as a photographer was made overnight.

VENTURE OF A LIFE-TIME

By the 1870s the railways had threaded their way across the country, and Bank Holidays and half-day Saturdays had been made obligatory by Act of Parliament. All of a sudden the working man and his family were able to enjoy days out, take holidays, and see a little more of the world.

With typical business acumen, Francis Frith foresaw that these new tourists would enjoy having souvenirs to commemorate their days out. For the next thirty years he travelled the country by train and by pony and trap, producing fine photographs of seaside resorts and beauty spots that were keenly bought by millions of Victorians. These prints were painstakingly pasted into family albums and pored over during the dark nights of winter, rekindling precious memories of summer excursions. Frith's studio was soon supplying retail shops all over the country, and by 1890 F Frith & Co had become the greatest specialist photographic publishing company in the world, with over 2,000 sales outlets, and pioneered the picture postcard.

FRANCIS FRITH'S LEGACY

Francis Frith had died in 1898 at his villa in Cannes, his great project still growing. The archive he created continued in business for another seventy years. By 1970 it contained over a third of a million pictures showing 7,000 British towns and villages.

Frith's legacy to us today is of immense significance and value, for the magnificent archive of evocative photographs he created provides a unique record of change in the cities, towns and villages throughout Britain over a century and more. Frith and his fellow studio photographers revisited locations many times down the years to update their views, compiling for us an enthralling and colourful pageant of British life and character.

We are fortunate that Frith was dedicated to recording the minutiae of everyday life. For it is this sheer wealth of visual data, the painstaking chronicle of changes in dress, transport, street layouts, buildings, housing, engineering and landscape that captivates us so much today, offering us a powerful link with the past and with the lives of our ancestors.

Computers have now made it possible for Frith's many thousands of images to be accessed almost instantly. The archive offers every one of us an opportunity to examine the places where we and our families have lived and worked down the years. Its images, depicting our shared past, are now bringing pleasure and enlightenment to millions around the world a century and more after his death.

The Villages

Most of the larger villages and towns of the Lake District occupy the most favoured sites in the valley bottoms, or command important river crossings. Although they may be small, many places have the urban air of small townships, which is exactly what they were in the days when the grant of a right to hold a market made the settlement, however tiny, an important trading centre for the surrounding countryside.

A family group of children enjoy a boating trip on the River Leven at Newby Bridge, at the southern end of Windermere. In the background is the 16th-century five-arched bridge which gave the village its name.

NEWBY BRIDGE

BY THE SWAN HOTEL

1914 / 67414

The name of this small settlement on the slopes of Wansfell Pike between Windermere and the Kirkstone Pass means exactly what it says —'the trout stream'—and it stands above a stream with the same name. At the south end of the village is Townend, a typical Lakeland statesman's house, now in the care of the National Trust.

TROUTBECK

GENERAL VIEW c1880 / 12522

The Troutbeck valley is one of the quietest in the Lake District, and in this view,
taken from the old coach route between
Windermere and Penrith, the essentially
rural nature of much of the district can
still be appreciated. The white-painted
farmhouse in the valley was probably
occupied by one of the district's famous
'statesmen' farmers.

TROUTBECK

THE VALLEY c1880 / 12523

Eamont Bridge, just south of Penrith on the A6, takes its name from this splendid three-arched bridge across the River Eamont. It is perhaps best known for its two prehistoric monuments: King Arthur's Round Table, a Bronze Age henge, and the former Neolithic stone circle and henge at Mayburgh, of which only one standing stone now remains.

EAMONT BRIDGE

1893 / 32934

The proprietress of Taylforth's Hotel (left), in the main street of Eamont Bridge, stands outside to bid farewell to a guest departing in a pony and trap. The photographer would certainly not be able to set up his tripod in the middle of the same street today!

EAMONT BRIDGE

THE HOTEL 1893 / 32932

CONISTON

THE PARISH CHURCH 1929 / 82799

This view from the church tower looks towards the wooded slopes of High Guards and up the valley of the Yewdale Beck. The whitewashed cottages of the village cluster around the church where the Yewdale Beck enters to the western side of Coniston Water.

CONISTON

FROM THE CHURCH TOWER 1906 / 54242

A pair of ramblers (right) heading for the hills stride out purposefully past the Rayburne Hotel and cafe in the centre of Coniston village. The lack of traffic in the main street is in sharp contrast with the scene today in this busy little village in the south-west Lakes.

CONISTON

THE VILLAGE 1929 / 82798

This general view of Ambleside, at the northern end of Windermere, was taken from the slopes of Loughrigg Fell. The spire of the parish church watches over this bustling village, which was founded in the 15th century; it once had thriving corn and bobbin mills on the River Rothay.

AMBLESIDE

FROM LOUGHRIGG 1892 / 30481

The umbrellas on the coach-and-four drawn up outside the ornate frontage of the Queen's Hotel appear to have been raised to protect the holders from the sun, rather than the rain. Other coaches wait for their passengers outside the other hotels for a day on the lakes.

AMBLESIDE

THE QUEEN'S HOTEL 1892/ 30484

AMBLESIDE

BRIDGE HOUSE 1912 / 64306

AMBLESIDE

THE WHITE LION AND ROYAL OAK HOTELS 1912 / 64303

We are in the centre of Ambleside; Lamb's Royal Oak Hotel is on the left, and the White Lion Hotel is in the centre. A coach-and-four has pulled up outside the White Lion, while bustle in the main street shows how busy Ambleside had become as a tourist centre by this time.

The Red Lion Hotel, on the right of the picture, gives its name to the square in the centre of the village, now dominated by traffic in a one-way system. The two cyclists meandering down the middle of the road would not be able to do so for long today!

GRASMERE

RED LION SQUARE 1926 / 79206

Church Stile is the name of the road which goes around the parish church. Notice the charming cottage draped with creeper opposite the churchyard with its unusual porch, and the village shop next to it. The shopkeeper is advertising flowers and plants of all kinds, including ferns and alpines.

GRASMERE

CHURCH STILE 1926 / 79208

William Wordsworth lived with his sister, Dorothy, at Dove Cottage, just outside the village, from 1799 to 1813. He wrote some of his best known poetry here. The cottage is now part of a museum dedicated to the life and work of the poet—the founder of the Lakeland Romantic Movement.

GRASMERE

WORDSWORTH'S COTTAGE 1936 / 87636

Horse-drawn coaches and a motor car are drawn up
outside the Rothay Hotel. The fast-growing tourist
trade made hotels such as this popular in the late
19th and early 20th centuries.

GRASMERE

THE ROTHAY HOTEL 1912 / 64338

The parish church of St Michael is one of the most interesting in the Lake District. It was originally built as a chapel in the 12th century; the present commanding building on its hill overlooking the village mainly dates from the 15th century. It contains Tudor murals and painted texts on its walls, and its parish registers go back to the same period. Hawkshead is one of the prettiest Lakeland villages; it stands at the head of Esthwaite Water, and was probably founded in the 10th century by a Norseman called Haukr.

HAWKSHEAD

THE PARISH CHURCH 1892 / 30534

A holidaying family relax with their dog outside the Old King's Arms pub and boarding house in the cobbled centre of the ancient village of Hawkshead. There have been a few changes here since the time of photograph no 38828: the gas lamp (left) has gone, the left-hand porch has been replaced, and the creeper on the centre porch seems to have migrated to the wall.

HAWKSHEAD

MARKET SQUARE 1929 / 82372

HAWKSHEAD

THE SQUARE 1896 / 38828

This picturesque cobbled square is in the centre of Hawkshead. An upended cart awaits its horse, while a little girl gazes across the empty square in anticipation. Now that most traffic by-passes this picturesque village, visitors can once again enjoy views like this, although it is seldom as quiet as here.

HAWKSHEAD

THE VILLAGE 1896 / 38831

William Wordsworth must have looked out from these mullioned windows of the ancient Grammar School, where he was educated between 1779 and 1787. The school, now a museum and library, sits comfortably beneath the bank on which the parish church of St Michael, seen in the background, stands.

HAWKSHEAD

THE GRAMMAR SCHOOL 1892 / 30538

HAWKSHEAD

FLAG STREET 1892 / 30537

There is not much traffic to be seen in Victoria Street at this time. Victoria Street leads off Church Street, now the A591, in this busy little town; it was originally known as Birthwaite, but it changed its name to match that of the nearby lake when the railway arrived in 1847.

WINDERMERE

VICTORIA STREET 1929 / 82818

Here we see the bridge over the River Greta in the busy little market town of Keswick in the northern Lakes. In the distance, on the left of the picture, can just be seen Greta Hall, former home of the poets Samuel Taylor Coleridge and Robert Southey. The pencil works of A Banks on the right is an example of one of Keswick's major industries, founded on supplies of plumbago, or black lead, from the Seathwaite valley in Borrowdale.

The Urban Scene

In a predominately rural area such as the Lake District, there are few towns. The major ones actually within the Lake District are Kendal (which has a separate chapter), Keswick and Windermere. Other towns on the fringe of the district include Cockermouth and Penrith. This section of photographs covers the urban aspect of the Lake District.

KESWICK

THE BRIDGE AND GRETA
HALL 1889 / 22086

33

Richard Rigg opened his Windermere Hotel in 1847—the same year as the Kendal and Windermere Railway reached the town—and his yellow-and-black coaches provided a connecting service from the adjacent station to various parts of the Lake District. The hotel is now known as the Windermere Hotel.

WINDERMERE

RIGGS HOTEL 1929 / 82820

Penrith received its first market charter in 1223, and it has continued as a busy market town serving the north-east of the Lake District and the North Pennines ever since. This view shows the Clock Tower and a surprisingly empty Market Place.

PENRITH

THE MARKET PLACE 1893 / 32923

The provision of the public gardens of the Promenade at Bowness also followed the coming of the railway in 1847, and the increased popularity of the Lake District as a health-giving holiday resort for people from the industrial towns and cities of the north west.

BOWNESS

THE PROMENADE 1925 / 77886

The Clock Tower which we saw in picture no 32923 (page 35) can just be seen in the background. Horse-drawn transport is obviously still in use, but it is about to be phased out by the motorised vehicles which were taking over the streets of the Cumbrian town.

PENRITH

CORNMARKET c1955 / P33013

We are looking down Penrith's main shopping street. The scene has not changed much since Victorian days, except for the fact that the horses have by now disappeared and have been replaced by motor vehicles.

PENRITH

KING STREET c1960 / P33023

Cockermouth is situated where the River Cocker joins the River Derwent on its way to the Irish Sea at Workington. This view looks across the Workington to Cockermouth railway line, which opened in 1847, towards the spire of the parish church of All Saints on the right.

COCKERMOUTH

GENERAL VIEW 1906 / 54987

The clock tower dominates the main street of the West Cumberland town. Cockermouth was granted its market charter in 1221, and gradually developed in importance until it was the chief commercial centre of the old county of Cumberland.

COCKERMOUTH

MAIN STREET 1906 / 54992

England's best known Romantic poet was born in this Georgian mansion in Cockermouth's Main Street in 1770. His father was steward to Sir James Lowther, and moved to the house in 1766. The house over-looks the River Derwent and has a delightful garden and terrace. It is now in the care of the National Trust.

COCKERMOUTH

WORDSWORTH'S BIRTHPLACE c1955 / C133005

Transport in the Lakes

The first tourists to the Lake District arrived by coach-and-four, and the most usual form of local transport was packhorse or horse and cart. By the time this collection of photographs were taken, the railway had arrived, but it was still to be many years before the Lakeland roads were to become choked with motor cars as they are today.

The Bowness Ferry across the narrowest part of the lake was originally a hand-rowed operation. But in 1870, twenty-six years before this photograph was taken, it became steam-operated. In this photograph, carts are being transported across the lake by the chain-operated pulley ferry.

WINDERMERE

THE FERRY BOAT 1896 / 38802

43

Another view of the Bowness Ferry shows a full coach-and-four just about to set out from the Bowness side of the lake, with the ferryman at the front steadying the nervous horses. This must have been a special trip, because by this time the sight of a coach-and-four was becoming increasingly rare.

WINDERMERE

THE FERRY BOAT 1896 / 38800

In the background is the Old England Hotel, one of many which sprang up in this little town as tourism took hold in the Lake District at the turn of the 19th century. The ivy-covered facade has not changed significantly.

BOWNESS

THE BOAT STATION AND THE OLD ENGLAND HOTEL 1893 / 31938

Organised sailing on Windermere started in the mid 19th century. The Windermere Sailing Club, later to become the Royal Windermere Yacht Club, was founded in 1860, and organised regular regattas on the lake. This photograph shows a regatta in progress near Bowness-on-Windermere.

WINDERMERE

SAILING BOATS 1896 / 38804

Horse-drawn coaches wait patiently to take passengers from the boats at Waterhead, near Ambleside on Windermere. The ornate Waterhead buildings served an increasing trade of tourists to the area, particularly after the railway came to the Lakes in 1847.

WINDERMERE

ABOVE WATERHEAD 1912 / 64319

Packed to the gunwales, the newly-commissioned pleasure steamer 'Teal' leaves Bowness Pier for a trip on Windermere. At this time, private boat ownership was beyond the means of all but the wealthiest visitors, so this was most people's only chance of enjoying the scenery from the lake.

BOWNESS

THE PLEASURE STEAMER 'TEAL' 1896 / 38795

Holidaymakers are boating on the southern reaches of Windermere near Newby Bridge. This is still a popular pastime on Windermere, which is England's largest lake; the calm reaches of the southern end of the lake provide a quiet backwater compared to the busy area around Bowness.

NEWBY BRIDGE

THE RIVER LEVEN 1914 / 67412

CONISTON

WATERHEAD 1912 / 64281

Waterhead on Coniston Water has not changed significantly since this photograph was taken. Even the elegant steam cruiser the 'Gondola', seen here moored at the pier, is still taking passengers up and down the lake. Originally built in 1859, it was rescued as a rotting hulk and restored to public use by the National Trust in 1980.

Carlisle and Sons' delivery van waits at the level crossing near Silecroft Station on the west coast route between Barrow and Workington, which opened to traffic in 1848. Silecroft, near Millom, stands at the southernmost extremity of the Lake District National Park, at the foot of Black Combe (1,970 ft).

SILECROFT

THE RAILWAY STATION c1950 / S657018

A steam train pulls into Newby Bridge Station, at the southern end of Windermere. The Ulverston to Lakeside line was built in 1869, but closed and then reopened again in 1965 as a tourist railway, known as the Lakeside and Haverthwaite Railway.

NEWBY BRIDGE

THE PLATFORM 1914 / 67417

Monuments and Houses

Probably because of its remoteness and lack of development, the Lake District is well-blessed with ancient monuments, from prehistoric stone circles and standing stones to the ruins of medieval castles. In addition, when the district became fashionable during the 18th and 19th centuries, the landed gentry chose it to build some of their most extravagant stately homes.

Just south of Penrith, Mayburgh Henge is a circular bank of earth and stones of about 1.5 acres, with one 10ft stone at the centre. It is thought to have been built between 1000BC-2000BC. There were four standing stones at the centre during the 19th century.

PENRITH

EAMONT BRIDGE

MAYBURGH HENGE 1893 / 32935

Erroneously known at the time when this photograph was taken as the Druids' Circle, the Castlerigg Stone Circle just outside Keswick is dramatically set in an amphitheatre of hills, including Skiddaw, seen in the background (left). It is thought to date from the Neolithic or early Bronze Age periods, predating the Druids by many centuries.

CASTLERIGG

THE DRUIDS' CIRCLE 1895 / 36951

Shap Abbey, near the banks of the River Lowther, was founded by the 'white canons' of the Premonstratensian order at the end of the 12th century, but it was dissolved, like so many others, in 1540. This photograph shows the imposing west tower, which was built about 1500, and which still stands almost to its full height.

SHAP

THE ABBEY 1893 / 32969

Kendal Castle was built by the Normans to the east of the town, probably by Ivo de Tailbois, the first Lord of Kendal in the late 12th century, and it still commands good views to the north and south-east. The castle was described as 'ready to drop down with age' by the beginning of the 17th century.

KENDAL

THE CASTLE 1894 / 34087

PENRITH

THE CHURCHYARD, THE GIANT'S GRAVE 1893 / 32926

Penrith Castle was built by William Strickland, later Bishop of Carlisle, who was given permission to build Penrith Castle in 1397, following the sacking of the town by raiding Scots in 1354. The curtain wall, shown in this photograph, is all that remains of Strickland's castle, which is now a public park.

PENRITH

THE CASTLE 1893 / 32928

The west wing of the original old hall at Holker, home of the Preston family since the 16th century, was destroyed by fire in 1871. This sumptuous rebuilding, supervised by the seventh Duke of Devonshire, was designed by Paley and Austin of Lancaster, and has been described as their most outstanding domestic work.

HOLKER HALL

1894 / 34106

The imposing red sandstone ruins of the keep of Brougham Castle watch over the River Eamont. Brougham Castle was originally built by the Normans, and was strengthened by Henry II in 1170. This was one of many castles to which Lady Anne Clifford, Countess of Dorset, made improvements, and she died here at the age of 90 in 1678.

PENRITH

BROUGHAM CASTLE 1893 / 32938

Cockermouth Castle was built in the 13th century on a strategic site to guard the confluence of the River Cocker and Derwent. Modifications, including a barbican and outer gatehouse, were made by Edward III in the 14th century, but the castle fell into ruin after a Civil War siege by Royalist forces in 1648.

COCKERMOUTH

THE CASTLE 1906 / 55001

The stately Gothic pile of Wray Castle can just be seen peeping over the trees in the background of this photograph, taken near its boathouse on the lake. Wray Castle was built by Dr James Dawson, a retired Liverpool surgeon, between 1840-7, and is one of the most extravagant of the 19th-century Lake District mansions. It is now a Merchant Navy training college.

WINDERMERE

WRAY CASTLE AND THE
BOATHOUSE 1886 / 18665

We are inside the three-sided court-yard of Sizergh Castle, near Kendal. Originally a 14th-century defensive pele tower, Sizergh was the home of the Strickland family; the present building is mainly a 15th-century Elizabethan mansion, now in the care of the National Trust.

SIZERGH CASTLE

1896 / 38542

LEVENS HALL

THE GARDENS 1891 / 28630

The Rural Scene

Outside the towns and villages of the Lake District, the rural scene had not changed much in many centuries. The small, isolated farmhouses and dalehead hamlets looked much as they had done since they were first established in the Middle Ages and before, as this selection of photographs shows.

Agriculture in the 1950s had not changed much since the 19th century, and horses were still commonly used on the land. This scene, showing the loading of a hay wagon on the shores of Buttermere, with Honister Crag and Fleetwith Pike prominent in the background, demonstrates that timeless way of life.

BUTTERMERE

HAYMAKING c1955 / B260064

The hamlet at the foot of Buttermere in the western Lake District takes its name from the lake; it is still the farming settlement it has always been. Buttermere takes its name from Old English, and means 'the lake by the dairy pastures'—where the butter is made. The farmstead of High Stile is still in the same business a thousand years later.

BUTTERMERE

HIGH STILE 1889 / 22065

BUTTERMERE

THE HOTEL c1873 / 6805

The small stock enclosure which goes across the Sail Beck was probably used for sheep washing in the summer, before shearing.

BUTTERMERE

THE VILLAGE 1889 / 22057

This very early postcard view of the Borrowdale Hotel, with Grange Crags behind, shows the Lake District as it was before the tourist invasion really took hold. The traffic-free minor road meanders south between drystone walls through the dale, towards Grange and Rosthwaite. The Borrowdale Hotel is in one of the wildest valleys of Lakeland. Early tourists were 'horrified' at the expanses of naked rock and impending mountains of places like Borrowdale, and feared to travel far into the dale, until poets like Wordsworth popularised the 'picturesque' mountain scenery.

BORROWDALE
THE HOTEL 1870 / 5047

Grange is the hamlet at the foot of Borrowdale, where the River Derwent, seen on the left of this photograph, meanders through water meadows into mighty Derwent Water to the north. The name 'grange' signifies an outlying farm, usually belonging to a monastery.

GRANGE-IN-BORROWDALE

1893 / 32887

The tiny church of St Olaf at Wasdale Head is said to be among the smallest in England; but surrounded as it is by the dramatic mountains of Wasdale, it is also one of the most visited. There are many memorials in the 400-year-old building to walkers and climbers who have met their deaths on England's highest hills.

WASDALE HEAD

ST OLAF'S CHURCH 1889 / 22075

The Bowder Stone, a 2,000-ton boulder which was transported to near Grange in Borrowdale by Ice Age glaciers, has been a source of tourist wonder for centuries. Today the stone is surrounded by trees; there is still a wooden staircase to reach the top.

BORROWDALE

THE BOWDER STONE 1893 / 32891

Wasdale and Wastwater can be said to have seen the birth of the sport of rock climbing, and climbers from all over Britain stayed at local hostelries such as the Victoria Hotel. Walter Haskett-Smith's first ascent of Napes Needle on Great Gable in 1886—only three years before this photograph was taken—is widely held to be the advent of the sport.

WASTWATER

THE VICTORIA HOTEL 1889 / 22077

LANGDALE

DUNGEON GHYLL FORCE 1888 / 20499

High Sweden Bridge is a picturesque packhorse bridge over the Scandale Beck between High Pike and Snarker Pike (there is a Low Sweden Bridge lower down the valley). It has no direct Scandinavian connection, other than the fact that the name comes from the Norse 'svithinn', which means 'land cleared by burning'.

AMBLESIDE

SWEDEN BRIDGE 1912 / 64330d

AMBLESIDE

THE STEPPING STONES 1888 / 20484

A crinoline-clad Victorian lady delicately picks her way across the stepping stones which cross the River Rothay, near Ambleside. Ladies were not seen in walking trousers or breeches in those days!

This is a classic view of Tarn Hows, near Hawkshead, with the peaks of the Langdale Pikes in the centre background. Despite its natural appearance, the lakes of Tarn Hows are in fact artificial, and there were once several smaller tarns. About 80 years ago, the landowner dammed the beck to create this familiar scene - one of the most visited places in the Lake District.

AMBLESIDE

TARN HOWS c1955 / A46145

Greenodd stands on the Leven Estuary where the River Leven from Windermere and the River Crake from Coniston Water flow into Morecambe Bay and the Irish Sea. The line of the Furness Railway, built in 1857, can be seen crossing the bay on the embankment to the right.

GREENODD

THE LEVEN ESTUARY 1921 / 70699

This is the original hand-rowed ferry service across the narrowest part of the Windermere at Bowness Nab. The lady in her long black dress and the gentleman wait for the ferryman to take them across to the western side of the lake, where the wooded Claife Heights stretch away to the right.

The Lakes

It is the lakes which give the Lake District its name, and they are what brings the majority of the tourists to the area. But there are several common misconceptions about them. There are actually only 16 lakes in the Lake District - and only one, Bassenthwaite, is actually called a lake. All the rest are 'meres' or 'waters', while the smaller mountain lakes are known as 'tarns'; they were all originally formed in troughs gouged out by Ice Age glaciers.

WINDERMERE

THE FERRY BOAT 1887 / 20461

The newly-built villas of Bowness-on-Windermere spread out towards the viewpoint of Biskey How in this view of the lake, looking towards the wooded island of Belle Isle, with the Claife Heights beyond.

WINDERMERE

FROM BISKEY HOW 1887 / 20438

A small boy in a rowing boat gazes at his reflection in the waters of Windermere in this summer photograph. The location is the Nickle Landing Stage, near Newby Bridge, at the southern end of the lake, where it narrows to enter the River Leven.

WINDERMERE

THE NICKLE LANDING STAGE 1914 / 67419

This view of Waterhead shows the Waterhead Hotel, built to serve the increasing numbers of tourists who were arriving by train at the lakeside station at Bowness, and catching a steamer up the lake to Waterhead.

WINDERMERE

THE WATERHEAD HOTEL 1887 / 20463

WINDERMERE

1886 / 18663

We are looking north from Lower Gatesgarth. The pines of Crag Wood are prominent in the centre of the photograph, while the slopes of Dodd sweep up the lake shore beyond. Buttermere and Crummock Water were once one large lake, until alluvium from Sail Beck gradually cut it in two. Gatesgarth is a place name which comes from Old Norse language, as do many in the higher hills of the Lake District. It means 'the pass where the goats go'.

BUTTERMERE

1889 / 22052

An Edwardian lady relaxes in a meadow on Colthouse Heights, on the eastern shores of Esthwaite Water, looking across to the knoll of Roger Ground, near Hawkshead. Esthwaite Water, south of Hawkshead, is one of the quietest of the lakes, and is a Norse name meaning 'the lake by the eastern clearing'.

ESTHWAITE WATER

ROGER GROUND FROM COLTHOUSE HEIGHTS 1912 / 64290

Seen on countless calendars, this view of Derwent Water from Ashness Bridge, on the narrow road up to Watendlath, is always popular. Skiddaw fills the backdrop. Cat Gill is the stream which plunges under the bridge on its way down to meet Derwent Water.

DERWENT WATER AND SKIDDAW

FROM ASHNESS BRIDGE 1893 / 32870

A picnic party in a meadow in the hamlet of Loweswater are enjoying the splendid view north up Crummock Water. The lower slopes of Grasmoor are prominent on the left, and the skyline is filled by Fleetwith Pike, Haystacks and High Crag. Rannerdale Knotts is the small dark hill in the middle distance above the lake.

CRUMMOCK WATER

FROM LOWESWATER 1889 / 22139

DERWENT WATER

THE RUSKIN MONUMENT, FRIAR'S CRAG 1906 / 54984

This is another of the Lake District's classic viewpoints, the backdrop formed by the peak of Causey Pike (2,035 ft). Friar's Crag is thought to have got its name as the embarkation point from monks visiting St Herbert on his island in the lake.

DERWENT WATER

FRIAR'S CRAG AND CAUSEY PIKE 1906 / 54982

This is an historic photograph of Thirlmere, taken from Hell How. It shows the last of the original two lakes—Leathe's Water and Wythburn Water—which formerly filled the valley below Helvellyn; they were joined and became the Thirlmere Reservoir when Manchester Corporation built the four-mile long reservoir between 1890-2.

THIRLMERE

FROM HELL HOW 1892 / 30562

This is one of the classic views of the Lake District; it is now used by the modern National Park Authority as its logo. This photograph of the northern shore of Wastwater shows (left to right) the trio of peaks at the head of England's deepest lake—Yewbarrow (2,061 ft), Great Gable (2,949 ft) and Lingmell (2,649 ft).

WASTWATER

THE LAKE 1889 / 22067

Ullswater snakes into the Lake District hills for seven and a half miles, from Pooley Bridge to Glenridding, and has three major and quite different stretches. This view, looking west from the slopes of Place Fell, is towards the head of the lake at Glenridding, and shows the northern stretch.

ULLSWATER

FROM PLACE FELL 1892 / 30548

This tranquil scene shows a rowing boat moored on the northern shore of Wastwater. The trees of Low Wood stretch out into the lake, while the steep scree-clad slopes of Illgill Head—the famous Wasdale Screes—soar up the southern shores.

WASTWATER

1889 / 22110

Stricklandgate, the northern extension of Highgate, is one of Kendal's main thoroughfares. The name means 'the road leading to the stirk land', and was often referred to as the Drover's Road, where cattle were driven from the north. This view, looking north, shows a traffic-free street.

The Town of Kendal

Kendal—the 'Auld Grey Town' on the River Kent—was founded on the wealth won from the wool of Lakeland sheep. Its motto is 'Pannis mihi Panis', which means 'wool is my bread'; even Shakespeare refers to Kendal Green cloth in Henry IV Part 1. But wool was not Kendal's only industry, and many other trades set themselves up in the many yards which lead off the main street of this southern gateway to the Lakes.

KENDAL

STRICKLANDGATE 1888 / 21088

This is a general view of Kendal from the south, with the Lakeland hills in the background. The town of Kendal was founded on the west bank of the River Kent, although the earliest settlement around the castle was on the east bank.

KENDAL

GENERAL VIEW 1896 / 38526

Kendal was granted the right to hold a market as early as 1189, when it was also made a barony. The Market Place had been enclosed on four sides until 1909, when it was opened to Stricklandgate, from where this view was taken. It shows the newly unveiled war memorial in the foreground.

KENDAL

THE MARKET 1924 / 75795

KENDAL

AN OLD YARD OFF STRICKLANDGATE 1914 / 67398

Here we see the lower or Nether Bridge across the River Kent. Now part of the one-way system, the Nether Bridge links the older, western side of Kendal with the newer, eastern suburbs. Miller Bridge, once known as Mill Bridge because it linked the mills on the east of the river with the town, is one of the chief bridges across the River Kent.

KENDAL

NETHER BRIDGE 1914 / 67381

KENDAL

HIGHGATE, 123 yard 1914 / 67393

KENDAL

STRAMONGATE, 59 yard 1914 / 67387

The County Hotel is one of the main hotels in the centre of Kendal; it dominates this part of the old town, whose wealth was founded on the woollen and textile industries. The famed Kendal bowmen at the Battle of Flodden Field (1513) were clad in home-spun Kendal Green cloth.

KENDAL

THE COUNTY HOTEL 1924 / 75801

The New Shambles, off Finkle Street, was built in 1803. The word 'shambles' comes from the Old English 'sceamol', which originally meant a bench for the sale of meat. The New Shambles replaced the Old Shambles, which was on the west side of Highgate. As we can see in this photograph, many types of shop occupied the units in the New Shambles.

KENDAL

THE NEW SHAMBLES 1914 / 67400

Branthwaite Brow is one of the three streets which meet Kent Street as it leads up the steep hill opposite Miller Bridge. The others are Finkle Street and Stramongate. This view looks down Branthwaite Brow towards the River Kent.

KENDAL

BRANTHWAITE BROW 1914 / 67383

KENDAL

SANDES HOSPITAL, GATEHOUSE, High Gate 1914 / 67385

111

The Fells and Passes

The earliest tourists to the Lake District were over-whelmed by the 'horrid' and 'frightful' nature of the mountains and crags, which frowned down on them as they negotiated the passes. It was Wordsworth and the other Romantic poets who first instilled the idea that the Lakeland fells had their own beauty and attractions, as generations of walkers and climbers have found since.

Grains Gill tumbles over a series of cascades beneath Stockley Bridge, near Seathwaite in Borrowdale, with Aaron Crags prominent on Seathwaite Fell in the background. The view is hardly changed today.

SEATHWAITE, STOCKLEY BRIDGE 1889 / 22017

HELVELLYN

STRIDING EDGE 1912 / 64342

Francis Frith's coachman takes a well-earned rest. His carriage has stopped near the summit of one of the most famous of the Lake District passes. It connects Troutbeck with Patterdale. The pass is said to have taken its name from a large rock which looks like a gable end of a church. This view looks south towards Troutbeck, with the shoulder of Broad End on the left.

KIRKSTONE PASS

c1870 / 5010

The Langdale Pikes are among the Lake District's most popular and recognisable hills. This view was taken from near the Dungeon Ghyll Hotel in Great Langdale, a popular starting point for walking the hills. Stickle Ghyll, which flows down from Stickle Tarn, passes under the bridge in this view, which looks towards the 2,403 ft summit of Harrison Stickle, the highest of the pikes.

LANGDALE PIKE

1892 / 30518

There is not much traffic—a car and a motorcycle with pillion passenger—in this view of the road running down from Dunmail Raise into Grasmere. The lake and village of Grasmere can be seen in the distance, while to the right, the 'Lion and Lamb' summit rocks of Helm Crag are seen silhouetted against the skyline.

GRASMERE VALE

1926 / 79213

A horse and cart wends its way up a gated minor road through the Coniston Fells. At the time before the coming of the motor car in significant numbers, there were many roads like this in the Lake District, and life continued among the hills at the same leisurely pace as it had for centuries.

CONISTON

THE FELLS 1912 / 64276

This view from Little Langdale looks towards Langdale Pikes, with the thimble-shaped Pike 'o' Stickle (2,323 ft) prominent on the left, and Gimmer Crag, and Harrison Stickle (2,403 ft) on the right in the distance. The slopes of Blake Rigg rise towards the left of the photograph.

LITTLE LANGDALE

1888 / 20495

Pike 'o' Stickle (2,323 ft) is the thimble-shaped peak prominent on the skyline in this view taken from near the head of Great Langdale. In the scree slope just visible below the summit of Pike 'o' Stickle, a pre-historic axe factory was discovered: here, the hard volcanic tuff was shaped into axes and transported all over Britain.

GREAT LANGDALE

1888 / 20497

INDEX